Acting Edition

The Thanksgiving Play

by Larissa FastHorse

SAMUEL FRENCH

ISBN 978-0-573-70785-8

www.concordtheatricals.com
www.concordtheatricals.co.uk

FOR PRODUCTION INQUIRIES

UNITED STATES AND CANADA
info@concordtheatricals.com
1-866-979-0447

UNITED KINGDOM AND EUROPE
licensing@concordtheatricals.co.uk
020-7054-7298

Each title is subject to availability from Concord Theatricals Corp.,
depending upon country of performance. Please be aware that *THE
THANKSGIVING PLAY* may not be licensed by Concord Theatricals
Corp. in your territory. Professional and amateur producers should
contact the nearest Concord Theatricals Corp. office or licensing
partner to verify availability.

MUSIC AND THIRD-PARTY MATERIALS USE NOTE

Licensees are solely responsible for obtaining formal written permission from copyright owners to use copyrighted music and/or other copyrighted third-party materials (e.g., artworks, logos) in the performance of this play and are strongly cautioned to do so. If no such permission is obtained by the licensee, then the licensee must use only original music and materials that the licensee owns and controls. Licensees are solely responsible and liable for clearances of all third-party copyrighted materials, including without limitation music, and shall indemnify the copyright owners of the play(s) and their licensing agent, Concord Theatricals Corp., against any costs, expenses, losses and liabilities arising from the use of such copyrighted third-party materials by licensees. For music, please contact the appropriate music licensing authority in your territory for the rights to any incidental music.

IMPORTANT BILLING AND CREDIT REQUIREMENTS

If you have obtained performance rights to this title, please refer to your licensing agreement for important billing and credit requirements.

THE THANKSGIVING PLAY premiered at Playwrights Horizons in New York City on October 12, 2018. The performance was directed by Moritz von Stuelpnagel, with scenic design by Wilson Chin, costume and puppet design by Tilly Grimes, lighting design by Isabella Byrd, and sound design by Mikaal Sulaiman. The production stage manager was Katie Ailinger, and the assistant stage manager was Jenny Kennedy. The cast was as follows:

LOGAN . . . . Jennifer Bareilles
JAXTON . . . . Greg Keller
ALICIA . . . . Margo Seibert
CADEN . . . . Jeffrey Bean

THE THANKSGIVING PLAY

was commissioned and originally produced by
Artists Repertory Theatre
Dámaso Rodriguez, Artistic Director Sarah Horton, Managing Director
Portland, Oregon

CHARACTERS

LOGAN – Female, Caucasian looking, the high school drama teacher that's always pushing the envelope in potentially inappropriate ways. Earnest about theatre and proving herself.

JAXTON – Male, Caucasian looking, yoga practitioner/actor. Politically correct to a fault, a big one. He's that confident guy everyone loves, but his logical PC thinking takes weird turns.

ALICIA – Female, brunette, Caucasian looking but has looks that would have been cast as ethnic in 1950s movies. Without guile. Sexy and hot, but not bright.

CADEN – Male, Caucasian looking, the academic. Awkward elementary school history teacher with dramatic aspirations but no experience.

SETTING

A high school drama classroom anywhere but the Los Angeles area.

AUTHOR'S NOTES

Scenes One, Three, Five, and Seven are sadly inspired by the Internet, mostly current teachers' Pinterest boards. Play with the theatricality of these scenes; perhaps children perform them, perhaps puppets, perhaps the actors as children, perhaps video, perhaps anything. Have fun.

For "**ALL**" cues, play with who says what. *Not* everyone says it together.

On casting: All ages are open and people of color that can pass as white should be considered for all characters.

Scene One

(Performers enter in school Thanksgiving outfits: Pilgrims, etc. They sing to the tune of "The Twelve Days of Christmas." Solos and movement encouraged.)

ACTOR. Www.childhood101.com/preschoolcountingsongs.

ALL.

ON THE FIRST DAY OF THANKSGIVING
THE NATIVES GAVE TO ME
A PUMPKIN IN A PUMPKIN PATCH.

ON THE SECOND DAY OF THANKSGIVING
THE NATIVES GAVE TO ME
TWO TURKEY GOBBLERS,
AND A PUMPKIN IN A PUMPKIN PATCH.

ON THE THIRD DAY OF THANKSGIVING
THE NATIVES GAVE TO ME
THREE NATIVE HEADDRESSES,
TWO TURKEY GOBBLERS,
AND A PUMPKIN IN A PUMPKIN PATCH.

ON THE FOURTH DAY OF THANKSGIVING,
THE NATIVES GAVE TO ME
FOUR BOWS AND ARROWS,
THREE NATIVE HEADDRESSES,
TWO TURKEY GOBBLERS,
AND A PUMPKIN IN A PUMPKIN PATCH.

ON THE FIFTH DAY OF THANKSGIVING,
THE NATIVES GAVE TO ME
FIVE PAIRS OF MOCCASINS,
FOUR BOWS AND ARROWS,
THREE NATIVE HEADDRESSES,
TWO TURKEY GOBBLERS,
AND A PUMPKIN IN A PUMPKIN PATCH.

ON THE SIXTH DAY OF THANKSGIVING,
THE NATIVES GAVE TO ME
SIX NATIVE TEEPEES,
FIVE PAIRS OF MOCCASINS,
FOUR BOWS AND ARROWS,
THREE NATIVE HEADDRESSES,
TWO TURKEY GOBBLERS,
AND A PUMPKIN IN A PUMPKIN PATCH.

ON THE SEVENTH DAY OF THANKSGIVING,
THE NATIVES GAVE TO ME
SEVEN NATIVE TOM-TOMS,
SIX NATIVE TEEPEES,
FIVE PAIRS OF MOCCASINS,
FOUR BOWS AND ARROWS,
THREE NATIVE HEADDRESSES,
TWO TURKEY GOBBLERS,
AND A PUMPKIN IN A PUMPKIN PATCH.

ON THE EIGHTH DAY OF THANKSGIVING,
THE NATIVES GAVE TO ME
EIGHT WOVEN BLANKETS,
SEVEN NATIVE TOM-TOMS,
SIX NATIVE TEEPEES,
FIVE PAIRS OF MOCCASINS,
FOUR BOWS AND ARROWS,
THREE NATIVE HEADDRESSES,
TWO TURKEY GOBBLERS,
AND A PUMPKIN IN A PUMPKIN PATCH.

ON THE NINTH DAY OF THANKSGIVING,
THE NATIVES GAVE TO ME
NINE CORNUCOPIAS,
EIGHT WOVEN BLANKETS,
SEVEN NATIVE TOM-TOMS,
SIX NATIVE TEEPEES,
FIVE PAIRS OF MOCCASINS,
FOUR BOWS AND ARROWS,
THREE NATIVE HEADDRESSES,
TWO TURKEY GOBBLERS,
AND A PUMPKIN IN A PUMPKIN PATCH.

ACTOR. Teacher's note: This song can do more than teach counting. I divide my students into Indians and Pilgrims, so the Indians can practice sharing.

Scene Two

(A high school drama classroom. It's bright and open with large recycling bins and a trendy water dispenser [alkaline, deionized, sewer; whatever is hippest]. The walls are lined with cast photos, Shakespeare pun posters, and funny props. The usual high school play posters are represented, along with some surprising ones like The Shipment, Extremities, *and* The Iceman Cometh.*)*

(Jaxton and Logan's clothes come from overpriced vintage/hip clothing stores where clothes from ten years ago are considered "retro." Alicia shops at Urban Outfitters with deliberate touches of money: Prada sunglasses, the "it" jeans of the moment, etc. Caden shops at The Gap. Banana Republic for something dressy. He carries a briefcase of papers.)

(Jaxton is purposefully never organized. He's on the floor, draped backward over a chair. Logan and Caden are institutionalized, they sit forward in chairs, although Logan fights it. All of them fall into yoga asanas from time to time, although Caden's aren't as skillful.)

(Occasional "snaps" from everyone.)

*(**JAXTON** and **LOGAN** set up the food table. **LOGAN** discovers a small cotton bag.)*

LOGAN. Is this for me?

JAXTON. Happy first day of rehearsal.

LOGAN. Jaxton, you didn't have to get me anything.

JAXTON. I know this gig is important to you so I want you to have something extra special.

(She opens the bag excitedly and pulls out...a mason jar.)

LOGAN. Oh. Wow. It's great.

JAXTON. It's a water bottle.

LOGAN. Sure.

JAXTON. It's made with recycled glass from broken windows in housing projects.

LOGAN. No way? That's amazing!

JAXTON. I know.

LOGAN. Where did you find it?

JAXTON. At the farmer's market. It's symbolic of the way we're gong to create this play. We start with this pile of jagged facts and misguided governmental policies and historical stereotypes about race then turn all that into something beautiful and dramatic and educational for the kids.

LOGAN. It's perfect. Thanks for getting me this gig. I'm not going to screw it up.

> *(They hug.)*
>
> (**JAXTON** *pulls out a wedge of cheese.*)

What's that?

JAXTON. What's what?

LOGAN. Is that soy cheese or coagulated cheese squeezed from a cow?

JAXTON. Coagulated.

You know I'm a vegan ally, but I've come to realize that I like cheese on my crackers.

LOGAN. I already struggle with the holiday of death.

JAXTON. If you're planning on "The Holiday of Death" as the title of our Thanksgiving play you'll lose your job for sure.

LOGAN. This is far more than a Thanksgiving play now. I got the Gender Equity in History grant, the Excellence in Educational Theater fellowship, a municipal arts grant and the Go! Girls! Scholastic Leadership mentorship.

JAXTON. I know parents, to get them back on your side, you need to kill a turkey.

LOGAN. I'm a vegan.

JAXTON. You're a teaching artist with a three hundred parent petition to fire you.

LOGAN. I am staying in the positive. This kind of talk isn't helping.

JAXTON. OK. Sending you nothing but light.

LOGAN. Thank you.

I have a surprise too. I also got that Native American Heritage Month Awareness Through Art grant.

JAXTON. Really?

LOGAN. They gave me funding so I could hire a professional actor.

JAXTON. Finally! Thank y–

LOGAN. And I was able to bring the perfect one to town. She elevates the whole project.

JAXTON. Professional actor right here.

LOGAN. Technically, you volunteer for these school plays.

JAXTON. I get paid for that show at the farmer's market.

LOGAN. Yeah but you do it on a street corner and are paid in a coffee can.

JAXTON. That is my official performance spot given to me by farmer's market security because they understand the importance of teaching about composting.

LOGAN. Jaxton, I value your work, but this woman is from Los Angeles.

JAXTON. Here we go with Los Angeles again. It's not the center of the acting world.

LOGAN. It kind of is.

JAXTON. The *commercial* acting world. Be grateful you didn't make it there. It shows what kind of person you are.

LOGAN. The kind of person who wasn't beautiful enough or sexy enough to compete?

JAXTON. Don't let your head go there Logan.

LOGAN. Well, wait until you see this actor. She's so beautiful. So LA.

JAXTON. What is beauty?

LOGAN. A social construct.

JAXTON. That we don't believe in. We value talent and art, not looks. You are a talented actress.

LOGAN. Even better, I'm a director now.

But I still let my past in LA color my present, don't I?

JAXTON. You can't reach new lands until you let go of the shore. Or in this case return to old lands, but as a more enlightened person because of the journey to the other land that was new but is now old and needs to be let go of.

LOGAN. Exactly. I think I can be a mentor to this woman. Help her recover from the false value placed on her sexuality because I've taken that journey. Show her how much more she can be. Thank you for that self-awareness.

JAXTON. You are one of the most self-aware people I know.

LOGAN. Since knowing you.

JAXTON. I just do my best and hope to Buddha that my karma makes up for the rest of it.

(They kiss.)

LOGAN. It's almost time for rehearsal. We should decouple.

(They separate and perform a decoupling ritual, moving from affection to neutral. This is a memorable movement that can be repeated whenever they get too personal.)

JAXTON. Nothing but gender-neutral actor, director respect from here on.

I'll get rid of the cheese.

LOGAN. No, I can handle it.

(CADEN enters.)

CADEN. Am I in the right place for rehearsal?

LOGAN. Welcome Mr. Green. I'm Logan, the director and your fellow collaborator.

CADEN. Please call me Caden. I'm only Mr. Green to my students.

LOGAN. This is Jaxton Smithton. Caden was generously assigned to us by the school district as our history specialist.

JAXTON. You're at Lincoln Elementary, right?

CADEN. I assure you my studies in American History go deeper than the elementary school level.

JAXTON. That's cool bro. We met at the Let's Learn! Science! tour. I was playing Einstein. You had the student that threw up on my shoes?

CADEN. Actually we met long before that. I've been to Let's Learn! Math! and Let's Learn! Geography! and all of the rest of the Let's Learn! tours.

JAXTON. I don't think we played at Lincoln on the Let's Learn! Math! tour.

CADEN. I took a personal day and saw it at Washington Elementary. I'm a huge fan of your work.
(*To* **LOGAN**.) And I've seen every show you've directed since you got to Jefferson High. *The Iceman Cometh* was made so much more relevant with fifteen-year-olds.

LOGAN. I appreciate that.

CADEN. It didn't deserve to be shut down.

LOGAN. Three hundred parents disagree.

JAXTON. For now.

LOGAN. I so appreciate your support Caden.

CADEN. I'm an amateur actor and writer on the side so it is a real thrill to work with professionals like yourselves.

JAXTON. That's awesome man. Us *professionals* welcome you.

CADEN. I'm especially excited because the email said this is a devised piece. So we're all contributing, right?

LOGAN. Yes. But as the director I have the final say in the construction.

CADEN. This is a dream come true for me.

LOGAN. I'm going to rely on you quite a bit. History is not my strength.

We're waiting on one more actor. Have some refreshments while I text her.

JAXTON. Some cheese Caden?

> (**LOGAN** *grabs her phone to text as* **ALICIA** *runs in. The men check her out.*)

ALICIA. So sorry I'm late. My Uber app disappeared and the place where I'm staying has terrible reception and I couldn't find the internet password so I had to take a bus. Have you ever taken a bus? It's impossible. I mean literally, it is not possible.

CADEN. I think the word you want is "figuratively" not "literally."

ALICIA. What?

CADEN. Because you're here. So it wasn't "literally" impossible. It's a common mistake.

ALICIA. Are you the director?

LOGAN. No, I am.

> (**ALICIA** *pointedly turns away from* **CADEN.**)

We met at your Skype audition.

ALICIA. I thought you were the casting director.

LOGAN. We don't have casting directors for elementary school shows. I'm the director director.

ALICIA. Oh. I'm Alicia *[Ah-lee-cee-a]*.

LOGAN. Yes, I remember. I hired you. I'm Logan. This is Caden and Jaxton.

ALICIA. Where's my script?

LOGAN. As my email said, we're devising the piece together. That's how I work.

ALICIA. I'm an *actress*.

LOGAN. We work as a team to come up with ideas, try them out, improv some scenes and then I put the connecting parts in and type it up.

ALICIA. Could I come back when there's a script? I just got to town and have a hundred things to do. And there's the bus. Figuratively.

CADEN. The bus itself is literal.

LOGAN. The devising process is meant to empower the actors.

ALICIA. Do I get paid extra for empowerment?

LOGAN. No. But I want you to know that your voice is the most important one in this play. More important than mine. We could not do this without you.

ALICIA. Really?

JAXTON. Really?

LOGAN. Absolutely. And personally, I'm here for you.

ALICIA. OK, I'll try it.

CADEN. Is this how you created all of your shows?

JAXTON. It's been a dream of ours to get to do a fully devised educational play. It's the wave of the future in theater. I mean actors in Sweden haven't touched a script in years. They're so far ahead of us.

ALICIA. IKEA is in Sweden right?

CADEN. Yes.

ALICIA. I love IKEA!

CADEN. Me too. Everything in my apartment is IKEA. Except my mattress and appliances. And the toilet. But everything else.

JAXTON. We all got sucked in, but now we realize what a huge environmental disaster it is to ship boxed packages all over the world when we can buy local.

CADEN. Oh. Yeah.

LOGAN. Anyway, let's get started.

CADEN. I combed through all of my research from grad school and came up with some ideas. Did my homework.

    (He chuckles.)

LOGAN. Let's start with your research then. Good drama is at its core, truth.

CADEN. I suggest we begin four thousand years ago when the ancient northern Europeans joined the agricultural revolution and reaped their first organized harvest as farmers. In order to give thanks to the gods for this new way of life they feasted with ceremonies. Thousands of years later those ceremonies become known as the modern Harvest Home Festival.

ALICIA. I thought we're doing a Thanksgiving play.

JAXTON. Another option is to focus on the fact that this is a November play.

ALICIA. Right. For Thanksgiving.

JAXTON. For Native American Heritage Month.

ALICIA. We're performing at something called the All School Turkey Trot. Not the Buffalo Teepee Trot.

JAXTON. It's not my place to tell you how to express yourself, but sound waves travel you know.

LOGAN. As our Native American compass, Alicia is allowed to say what she wants about it.

(**ALICIA** *flips her hair.*)

JAXTON. Native American?

LOGAN. I told you we got that Heritage Month grant. To hire the professional actor.

JAXTON. You didn't say it was for a Native American actor.

LOGAN. I thought it was implied.

JAXTON. *(To* **ALICIA.***)* I'm so sorry. It is truly an honor to work with you. I have always been drawn to your ways.

ALICIA. You're a fan of my work?

JAXTON. More than a fan. I'm a devoted follower.

ALICIA. That's sweet. I just opened a new Instagram account. You should follow that one too.

JAXTON. I will.

LOGAN. Now is a good time to mention that in the interest of full disclosure, there are many factors, grant and school board requirements that we need to fulfill with this piece, including Thanksgiving. I am a vegan so that subject is especially sensitive for me. However I want to lift up the acknowledgement that although my sensitivity about the slaughter of millions of animals, including forty-five million turkeys, is valid, I am conscious of not allowing my personal issues to take up more space in the room than the justified anger of the Native people around this idea of Thanksgiving in our post-colonial society. I want to make that crystal clear. Especially for you Alicia.

ALICIA. Um...OK.

LOGAN. If there is anything you want to say on the subject, please know we are holding that space for you.

ALICIA. I'm good right here.

LOGAN. OK. This bit of research is great Caden and helps fulfill my Excellence in Education grant. But I wonder if the best place to start a forty-five minute Thanksgiving play for elementary grades is four thousand years ago?

ALICIA. Yeah, America didn't even exist.

JAXTON. Better times. That makes me wonder if using the word of the conqueror, "American," could be a trigger for people? What word do you prefer for naming this physical space? I've heard "Turtle Island" used a lot. Do you prefer that?

ALICIA. I like turtles.

LOGAN. Thanks for lifting up that awareness Jaxton. Coded language is an issue we need to be conscious of, especially when dealing with the next generation.

ALICIA. I don't get codes.

JAXTON. Because that's Navajo.

CADEN. My next idea is pretty cool. Harvest Home Festival is a direct line that can easily be drawn to our modern Thanksgiving celebration. See I propose that we open on a huge bonfire with ancient Northern European ancestors dancing and feasting on one side and – this is the exciting part – ancient Native American people doing the exact same thing on the other side!

ALICIA. I don't get it.

CADEN. Of course they weren't called "Native American" then. Coded language, thank you Alicia. We show that both these cultures were already celebrating harvests on both sides of the Atlantic. Two peoples on a parallel track for centuries before they collided as settlers and Wampanoags. History is so dynamic. I mean it's really perfect for theater.

LOGAN. Yes. It is. I'm feeling your passion and I love that. But here's the reality, it's just the three of you.

CADEN. OK.

LOGAN. And it's a school show. Like all the other ones you've seen. So...fire won't fly.

CADEN. Then I'm not clear how you plan to depict anything, even up to the "traditionally" recognized Thanksgiving, since all of their lighting, cooking and warmth was fire.

LOGAN. We're going to have to imagine that part.

CADEN. But your email said we are going to do something revolutionary in educational theater.

JAXTON. We're aiming for a revolution of ideas.

CADEN. So, we open on the two civilizations having feasts on opposite sides of...the imaginary fire?

LOGAN. Let's put that in the simmering pot for now.

CADEN. But to make it simmer –

LOGAN. Let's move forward in history. What can we do to break down the myths and stereotypes of Thanksgiving in forty-five minutes with three people? Create a revolution in their minds?

ALICIA. Forty-five minutes seems kinda long.

LOGAN. Well, it's a play. So actually it's quite short.

ALICIA. But an average show at Disneyland is twenty minutes. That's what they think kids can handle.

LOGAN. Um, we can consider that point of view but I don't think Disney –

ALICIA. If anyone knows kids, it's Disneyland. It's like science to them. I know, I was the third understudy for Jasmine.

JAXTON. Isn't she Middle Eastern?

ALICIA. My look is super flexible.

JAXTON. Oh yeah, I totally get that.

LOGAN. I hear you Alicia, but the standard commission from this school district is for a forty-five minute show, so we should probably trust that they know a little something about children. Even if they do feed them slaughtered flesh and genetically enhanced garbage every day.

ALICIA. I guess.

LOGAN. Caden, what can you tell us about the first recognized Thanksgiving in America?

CADEN. I imagined the third scene three thousand and five hundred years after the first.

LOGAN. What year?

CADEN. 1565.

LOGAN. That sounds close.

CADEN. In Saint Augustine, Florida.

ALICIA. The Pilgrims landed in Florida? I did not know that. So that's why Disney World is there? Because it was the original crossroads of the world?

CADEN. Saint Augustine was a settlement of hundreds of Spanish people led by Pedro Menéndez.

ALICIA. I might be a little bit Spanish! Para Español, oprima numero dos.

CADEN. This Thanksgiving was a mass to celebrate a safe journey. Pedro ordered that the Native people be fed as an act of good will. Fun fact. Because they just came from Puerto Rico, it is likely that there were tropical fruits at the first feast instead of yams and squash.

JAXTON. So you want us to celebrate Native American Heritage Month with a play about Spanish people holding a Catholic mass and eating pineapples?

CADEN. That's just one scene.

LOGAN. The missionaries, Catholicism specifically, are difficult subjects for Indigenous people.

CADEN. But it's true.

JAXTON. Seriously?

LOGAN. Can we jump ahead to New England?

CADEN. But the scene of the next recognized Thanksgiving happens thirty years later in Texas.

ALICIA. OMG. There were Pilgrims in Texas too?

CADEN. An expedition of 500 Spanish people crossed the desert from Mexico to Texas. Men, women, children and animals died along the way. Finally, they made it to the Rio Grande. However, many of the people were so overcome with excitement to find water that they rushed into the river and drowned.

JAXTON. Gotta admit, did not see that coming.

CADEN. Those that remained, gave thanks.

LOGAN. How is this appropriate for children?

CADEN. The local Indigenous people joined them and caught fish for the feasting.

LOGAN. From the Rio Grande?

CADEN. I assume so.

ALICIA. Ew.

CADEN. People in El Paso still celebrate that feast as the first Thanksgiving. Only it's in April.

LOGAN. Caden, are we getting close to the normal Thanksgiving? The relatively happy one? In November.

CADEN. That's my next series of proposed scenes. But I warn you, there is drama galore. At least four different dates are vying for the privilege of being "first." And the reasons behind the feast are incredibly varied. From the gruesome –

LOGAN. Worse than eating fish that ate your drowned friends?

CADEN. Much worse. To speculation that the entire Thanksgiving story is a fiction concocted to celebrate the victory of capitalism over communism.

JAXTON. So far all of these stories are coming from the non-Indigenous point of view. I think we need to hold space for the Native perspective.

ALICIA. That's my role.

LOGAN. Alicia, what were you told about the first Thanksgiving in your family?

ALICIA. Well, not much really. I mean we aren't religious or anything.

JAXTON. Of course not.

ALICIA. We just ate food and watched games. We didn't talk about it much.

LOGAN. Maybe we could do something with that? Use play as a universal way to connect with the kids instead of those tired children's songs we make them sing every year.

JAXTON. What kinds of games?

ALICIA. Just the ones that everyone watches.

LOGAN. Right. Is there any chance we could learn about these games with you, as a cast?

ALICIA. I guess. I think the Chiefs are playing Monday, right?

JAXTON. There's a whole game just for chiefs? That's amazing. How many are there?

ALICIA. The same number as any team I guess. I don't really know football that well. It was just on in the background.

JAXTON. Wait, football?

ALICIA. Sure. What do you watch?

(They laugh uneasily.)

LOGAN. NFL football. Well, not anymore, but...

JAXTON. This is a perfect example of the exotification of your people. We assumed that you were watching Native American lacrosse or something instead of allowing you to just be contemporary people. Of course your family watched football. Whose didn't?

CADEN. Mine didn't.

LOGAN. I can't believe we did that. Sorry Alicia.

ALICIA. We did do one different thing on Thanksgiving. It came from my mom's people.

LOGAN. Do you mind sharing it with us?

JAXTON. Maybe we could get permission to incorporate it into the play? Respectfully.

ALICIA. First we'd buy an extra frozen turkey, a small one, and leave it in the freezer. Then before dinner all the kids would go out to the driveway and set up these wood blocks like bowling pins. Then we'd take turns rolling the frozen turkey at the pins and see who could knock down the most.

JAXTON. Like bowling?

LOGAN. With a frozen turkey?

ALICIA. Yeah that's what they called it, Frozen Turkey Bowling. It was hilarious. Your hands would be freezing so you'd just chuck the thing and it would go all over the driveway. They call them Butter Balls, but really, they're not shaped like balls.

LOGAN. This is your family tradition?

ALICIA. My mom grew up in Iowa, so it probably worked better there because it was cold. In LA it would start melting and get all mushy and runny.

(**LOGAN** *looks like she is going to puke.*)

LOGAN. Oh my God.

JAXTON. Deep breaths.

LOGAN. We really want to honor your voice and your people's. I just realized that I never asked who your people are.

ALICIA. Um...you mean my family?

LOGAN. What are they called?

ALICIA. Well my dad's side is the Longs and my mom's is Hogan. But I use my middle name as my last name for acting. It makes it so I can play all kinds of people.

JAXTON. Can I ask something in all respect?

ALICIA. I guess.

JAXTON. Isn't that problematic? I mean we're all becoming aware of redface. Doesn't it worry you to be playing other races?

ALICIA. My agent had me take headshots as six different ethnic people, which got me many roles such as Jasmine.

JAXTON. How do you even take headshots as ethnicities? What does that look like?

ALICIA. Different hair, accessories. My Native American shot has me in braids and a turquoise necklace.

JAXTON. Native Americans need to take "Native American" headshots? That seems wrong.

ALICIA. Every actress in LA has different types of shots. My agent told me to.

LOGAN. I wouldn't do everything your agent says.

ALICIA. He's my former agent now so I don't do anything he says. Besides Native Americans like invented turquoise so I don't see why wearing it in a shot would piss them off. It's paying them respect.

LOGAN. Them who?

ALICIA. The Native Americans.

LOGAN. But you're them.

ALICIA. Who?

LOGAN. Native American.

ALICIA. I *play* Native American.

JAXTON. You're not Native American?

ALICIA. I'm English and French and a little Spanish we think.

LOGAN. But I hired you to be the Native American.

ALICIA. Yeah.

LOGAN. But you aren't?

ALICIA. No.

LOGAN. But you were my cultural compass.

ALICIA. You hired me to be an actress. Don't worry, I'm gonna act my ass off.

LOGAN. But that's why your voice was so important.

ALICIA. My voice is the most important. You said so.

LOGAN. Because I thought you were Native American.

ALICIA. So non-Native American voices aren't important?

JAXTON. Didn't you wonder why we were asking your advice on all of this stuff?

ALICIA. Because it's *devised*.

LOGAN. But we need a Native American person to do this play. I got a grant.

ALICIA. Look, you hired me off my Native American headshot, so that's on you. You can't fire me because of this. It's a law.

LOGAN. So we're four white people making a culturally sensitive First Thanksgiving play for Native American Heritage Month? Oh my Goddess.

(JAXTON *reaches out to comfort her, she pulls away.*)

ALICIA. Whatever, it's theater. We don't need actual Native Americans to tell a Native American story. I mean, none of us are actual Pilgrims are we?

CADEN. Interestingly they didn't call themselves Pilgrims at all. That's a name given to them –

ALICIA. The point is, we're actors. We act. That's the job. Is Lumière a real candlestick?

JAXTON. Actually he kind of was.

ALICIA. Was Grandmother Willow a real willow?

CADEN. She's animated so –

ALICIA. In the Disneyland show?

CADEN. No?

ALICIA. Exactly. And that whole Pocahontas cast was Filipino. We shared a green room.

JAXTON. Do you have any non-Disney references in your life?

LOGAN. I could lose my job over this.

CADEN. I don't think that Alicia playing Native will be a problem with the school district. There are schools that are nearly all black, all Hispanic. If they tried to find ethnic-specific roles for everyone to play, they wouldn't be able to produce anything.

LOGAN. I know about color-blind casting, Caden, I'm the drama teacher. There are grants at stake! A lot of them. And the petition! If I'm not a director or an educator I'm...nothing.

I'm –

JAXTON. Lo, stay in *this* moment.

LOGAN. But this moment sucks. Take five!

(Everyone disperses.)

Scene Three

(Perhaps as turkeys, perhaps not. Can be sung or recited.)

ACTOR. A selection from songsforteachers.org.

ALL.

FOUR LITTLE TURKEYS STANDING IN A ROW.
FIRST LITTLE TURKEY SAID, "I DON'T WANT TO GROW."
SECOND LITTLE TURKEY SAID, "WHAT DO YOU KNOW?"
THIRD LITTLE TURKEY SAID, "THANKSGIVING IS NEAR."
FOURTH LITTLE TURKEY SAID, "YES, THAT'S WHAT I HEAR."

THEN THE FOUR LITTLE TURKEYS
THAT WERE STANDING IN A ROW,
ALL SAID TOGETHER...
"COME ON, LET'S GO!"

TWO LITTLE INDIANS FOOLIN' WITH A GUN,
ONE SHOT T'OTHER AND THEN THERE WAS ONE;

ONE LITTLE INDIAN LEFT ALL ALONE;
HE WENT OUT AND HANGED HIMSELF
AND THEN THERE WERE NONE.

FOUR FAT TURKEYS SITTING ON THE GATE.
THE FIRST ONE SAID, "OH MY, IT'S GETTING LATE!"
THE SECOND ONE SAID, "THANKSGIVING IS OUR FATE."
THE THIRD ONE SAID, "HERE COMES THE FARMER WITH
    HIS GUN!"
ALL SAID TOGETHER...
"RUN, RUN, RUN!"

(They scatter. Bam! Bam! Bam! As each gunshot is heard another turkey "dies." One is left alone. She dodges right, left, ducks, and finally...Bam! She's down.)

ACTOR. Teacher's comment: For fun, try having students sing "Injun" instead of "Indian." My students loved it.

Scene Four

(**ALICIA** *and* **CADEN** *have snacks.*)

CADEN. So you just moved here?

ALICIA. Yeah.

CADEN. What part of town are you in?

ALICIA. I don't know.

CADEN. I grew up here. If you want to know anything about anything I can probably tell you.

ALICIA. Anything?

CADEN. Anything about this town.

ALICIA. Oh.

CADEN. But if there's anything else you want to know about I could look it up for you. I'm really good at research.

ALICIA. That's sweet.

CADEN. Do you want my number or whatever?

ALICIA. I don't know if I'll be here long.

CADEN. Don't like to count your chickens before they hatch?

ALICIA. I thought we're doing turkeys.

> (*She eats her snacks, then looks at the ceiling.*
> **CADEN** *goes over his notes.*)

> (**JAXTON** *joins* **LOGAN.**)

LOGAN. I've already screwed this up.

JAXTON. We can fix it. I looked over your Native American Heritage Month grant and it doesn't explicitly say you have to use it for a Native American person.

LOGAN. Really?

JAXTON. As long as we do something that honors Native Americans for November, you're good to keep the money.

LOGAN. That doesn't seem right. Besides I really wanted to have a Native American voice in this play.

JAXTON. Didn't you check her enrollment card or something?

LOGAN. It's illegal to ask about ethnic, gender or religious identification in the hiring process. Which I totally support.

JAXTON. But it was pretty obvious that she's not Native.

LOGAN. You thought she was.

JAXTON. I could tell something was off. She's not centered enough.

If it's so important to you, we can add a Native actor. A real one.

LOGAN. None applied.

JAXTON. I find it hard to believe there aren't any Native American actors around here.

LOGAN. Have you ever seen one? I don't have the time or resources to go door to door to find one. Alicia cost a lot of money.

It's harder to be a mentor to her than I thought it would be.

JAXTON. She does have a ton of conventional beauty and sex appeal.

LOGAN. Jaxton!

JAXTON. I'm not saying I'm into that, but she has a lot to overcome. It will take time.

LOGAN. Despite all that, do you think we could still use her as Native American and call it color-blind casting?

JAXTON. I think we could get away with using her a few years ago, but now we're post the post-racial society. We can't be blind to differences.

LOGAN. Right. Before we were blind to race but now we totally see it. It's our duty as allies.

JAXTON. Yes. And as allies we need to say something for those who can't be here to speak for themselves.

LOGAN. Or, is it as allies we need to be sure they are here to speak for themselves?

JAXTON. That's what I'm saying.

LOGAN. So if they aren't here, does anyone speak for them?

JAXTON. I don't think we're supposed to speak for anyone but ourselves.

LOGAN. Right. So we just speak for white people?

JAXTON. I think so. We see color but we don't speak for it.

LOGAN. Which means Alicia can't play Native American, for sure?

JAXTON. Definitely not.

LOGAN. But can we really say that? Then we're speaking for Native American people who aren't here.

JAXTON. Maybe we should tell a Native American person and see if they say it.

LOGAN. Yes of course.

    (Thinks.)

But I don't know any Native Americans.

JAXTON. A guy in my yoga class built a sweat lodge on his deck so he probably knows a local Native American person. He made it totally traditional.

LOGAN. That means he used dead animal skin to cover it didn't he?

JAXTON. Yes, but it's all upcycled leather from jackets he gets on Etsy.

LOGAN. That helps.

But you friend's not Native American?

JAXTON. No, he learned how to build it at Burning Man. But I'm sure he's had a Native American person to the lodge. Wait, he's at a yoga retreat in Machu Picchu. No phones allowed.

LOGAN. Well then, I guess in the absence of any Native American people, we should make a decision, for the good of the school system, so they don't get in trouble.

JAXTON. Right, then we're technically still speaking on behalf of white people because we're speaking for the school administration.

LOGAN. Yes. That sounds right. We're white people speaking for white people.

JAXTON. OK.

LOGAN. We can do that.

JAXTON. Absolutely.

LOGAN. *(To the group.)* We're back people. After some thinking I have decided that we cannot use non-Native American people to play Native American characters.

CADEN. So there won't be any Native Americans in a Thanksgiving play for Native American Month?

JAXTON. It's the right thing to do.

ALICIA. What part will I play?

LOGAN. A pilgrim.

ALICIA. But I'm maybe part-Spanish so I should have the biggest parts in the Florida and Texas stories.

LOGAN. We aren't going to do those stories.

ALICIA. Why not?

CADEN. Yes, why not?

LOGAN. Because there aren't any white people in them and we've got a cast of white people.

ALICIA. In this country if you're part anything else, you're not white. It's a drop thing.

(To **CADEN.***)* If I'm Spanish I'm not white, right?

CADEN. I think that depends on the region of origin. I'm not an expert on –

*(***ALICIA** *gives him a look.)*

I'll do the research and get back to you.

LOGAN. The ethical thing to do is to play what we know we are.

ALICIA. I was promised a large part.

LOGAN. My Gender Equity in History grant requires a lead female historical figure, so that will be you.

ALICIA. Good.

LOGAN. This is a challenge, but we are the future of theater and education. Are we all in agreement?

JAXTON. Support.

ALICIA. *Main* pilgrim.

LOGAN. Yes. Caden?

CADEN. I'll defend you to the school board if I have to.

LOGAN. OK then, no Native Americans in our Thanksgiving play.

Let's start with an improv. We'll use the traditional story we all know. Just see where it goes.

CADEN. That story isn't necessarily historically accurate.

LOGAN. We need to get our creative juices flowing and figure out what our options are to celebrate Native Americans without them. Let's act.

> *(JAXTON, ALICIA, and CADEN turn in circles a bit, not sure where to face.)*

ALICIA. Which way is downstage?

LOGAN. It doesn't matter in an improv. You just react.

> *(They wander a bit, not able to define a space.)*

Let's put the audience here.

> *(They all face LOGAN downstage and fall into line.)*

You're at a pilgrim's house preparing the meal for the first Thanksgiving.

> *(They move chairs around.)*

ALICIA. I feel like it's my house.

LOGAN. Fine. Let's leave the rest of the discoveries for the improv.

> *(They mime preparing foods. Perhaps too graphically.)*

JAXTON. Wait. Didn't we get this food from Native American people?

ALICIA. Yeah, isn't that the whole point of Thanksgiving? To thank the Native people for saving us from... something...with food?

CADEN. Starvation.

ALICIA. We should totally thank them for that.

JAXTON. Why are we fixing this food if it was a gift?

LOGAN. The Pilgrims must have done some of the actual preparation.

JAXTON. But without any Native American people to guide them?

CADEN. Actually –

LOGAN. OK, you're sitting down to eat the dinner that is already prepared.

> (ALICIA *sits across from* JAXTON *and* CADEN. *They mime eating. Have fun.*)

ALICIA. Would you like more stuffing?

CADEN. Stuffing is a modern dish. A more likely side considering the efficiency of the early settlers would be a type of sweetbreads or pate.

LOGAN. Caden, we call improv a world of yes. We don't judge or try to make sense of choices, we simply say "yes" and see where it leads us.

CADEN. So sorry.
> (*To* ALICIA.) Yes, I would love some, what did you call it? Stuffing?

ALICIA. I was mistaken. It's corn. Native American corn.

CADEN. Thank you.

JAXTON. This meal is wonderful.

ALICIA. Without our Native American neighbors...in the next room, we would be dead. From starvation.

CADEN. (*Pleased.*) Yes. We owe them thanks.

ALICIA. I thanked them.

JAXTON. Good.

> (*They mime-eat in silence. For awhile.*)

ALICIA. We should say a prayer of Thanksgiving.

LOGAN. Public schools.

ALICIA. What?

LOGAN. We can't pray in public schools.

ALICIA. (*To* CADEN.) Pilgrims are religious. Right?

CADEN. Yes!

ALICIA. Brother Jaxton, would you say a prayer of thanks?

JAXTON. O...K. Um... Dear... Father. Shouldn't we wait to say the prayer until our Native...um...brothers – What should we call them?

LOGAN. Indigenous people?

CADEN. The truth is in the writings from this time, they were referred to as "savages." But we can't say that in a school show. We could call them "the Natives." As in they are native to this land.

JAXTON. OK. But my point was going to be, we should have our Native brothers in the room to say the Thanksgiving prayer.

ALICIA. Yes. Let's wait for them. More...vegetable?

CADEN. Thank you.

(*More mime. Silence.*)

LOGAN. And scene. We can't pray, and we can't do a hero story without the hero.

JAXTON. It's weird.

CADEN. Somehow we need Indians.

(*They think.*)

ALICIA. A dream sequence.

JAXTON. How does that help?

ALICIA. My character can dream that she is a Native person. And I'll play me because it's my dream.

CADEN. I think that's still redface.

ALICIA. I'm not Native. I'm a pilgrim dreaming Native. It's totally different.

CADEN. Well...

JAXTON. Technically she would still be in redface, but we're not hiding that she's in redface.

LOGAN. It's meta, so maybe it's OK.

JAXTON. I think so.

ALICIA. Why are you the ones who get to decide everything?

LOGAN. As enlightened white allies, Jaxton and I have put a lot of thought into these issues.

JAXTON. Like every day of our lives. We can't escape our whiteness.

ALICIA. But I play white. I can decide things too.

JAXTON. Yeah but I'm a straight. White. Male. It's an endless minefield.

CADEN. I'm straight too. Funnily I am Italian which used to be considered ethnic but is now white.

JAXTON. Whoa, this whole thing must be bringing up a lot of sensitivity issues for you. For being one of Christopher Columbus's bros.

CADEN. I'm not related to Columbus.

JAXTON. But you have the awareness that your people started the slavery and genocide of millions.

CADEN. That's not all Columbus did.

JAXTON. You're balancing karma. We uplift the celebration of Native American Heritage Month and Columbus Day inches a little closer to oblivion.

CADEN. Well, Columbus Day is actually a celebration of the contributions of Italians to –

JAXTON. Then why not Mussolini Day? Or –

LOGAN. Focus people. The new idea on the table is that Alicia will dream that she is Native American, thus allowing a Native point of view in the piece. Do we have consensus?

JAXTON. I guess.

CADEN. Yes.

ALICIA. You know what would be great? If it was like me talking to myself. Like Native me talking to Pilgrim me. Helping me see the beauty and bounty of this land.

> (**JAXTON** *pulls out his phone and looks at it through the following.*)

LOGAN. So you are proposing that this whole section is just you?

ALICIA. I can tell the other characters about my dream in the morning.

LOGAN. Then it's just monologues.

ALICIA. Some amazing plays are mostly monologues. Like *The Vagina Monologues.*

CADEN. As an elementary school teacher I can say with authority that monologues put children to sleep. Sorry.

JAXTON. What we need is conflict. I was just googling and things weren't so chill between the Pilgrims and the Indians. I mean, obviously, the Pilgrims were land stealers like Columbus. But they were totally in the middle of some very specific battles.

ALICIA. So you guys can battle Native me in my dream.

JAXTON. Or we can all be white people, Pilgrims, preparing for a battle. War is intense. Kids dig that.

CADEN. I brought a dramatic, post-battle scene that only involves white people, technically.

JAXTON. Sweet.

LOGAN. We're celebrating violence?

JAXTON. Maybe my character is conflicted about fighting the Indians.

(*To* **ALICIA.**) Good wife, I'm so conflicted about the impending war.

(*She slides up next to him, very cozy.*)

ALICIA. Let me soothe you, dear husband.

LOGAN. Maybe she's your sister! Or your platonic friend?

ALICIA. Oh, you're a couple. I did not get that.

LOGAN. Jaxton and I share a mutually respectful relationship.

ALICIA. So you aren't a couple?

LOGAN. New plan. We are going to divide and conquer. Sorry. Alicia and I will work on her dream idea. Jaxton and Caden work on the battle idea.

JAXTON. Wait. Isn't it inappropriate for us to split along gender lines?

CADEN. I'll work with Alicia.

LOGAN. But is it more inappropriate for us to intentionally not split along gender lines?

JAXTON. I don't know.

LOGAN. The impetus was creative interest, so I think it's OK.

JAXTON. But two men doing the war stuff? Isn't that playing into gender assumptions that we want to disrupt?

LOGAN. But it's period so we're being historically accurate.

JAXTON. Right.

LOGAN. Yes.

JAXTON. Sorry.

LOGAN. No, thanks for always being conscious.

CADEN. Are there any props or costumes here?

LOGAN. There's a few.

JAXTON. *(To* **CADEN.***)* The good stuff is out in the storage closet. Come on.

CADEN. Great.

(The men go.)

LOGAN. Alicia, I want to be sure there are no hard feelings in what just happened with the Native American casting, redface thing. I don't blame you at all, and I hope you understand why we had to make this decision.

ALICIA. You're the director, it's your show.

LOGAN. No, it's our show. Really. I want you to feel as empowered as possible. I've been a female actor in LA.

ALICIA. You lived in LA?

LOGAN. For six weeks. My time in LA was…hard. But since then I've seen how it's not us, as women, but the business that makes us believe in the lies of beauty and sex.

ALICIA. But sex is a real thing.

LOGAN. Yes, but believing that your value is tied to your ability to portray sex and beauty is a lie.

ALICIA. You don't think I'm beautiful?

LOGAN. Well, yes. In the way our society defines beauty and attaches worth to it. I realize now that my own beauty is from the inside. We are all beautiful.

ALICIA. Of course you are.

LOGAN. You see my inner beauty?

ALICIA. No. I mean you're really pretty. You just hide it. But I could help you. It would only take a little makeup to highlight your eyes and add some lift to your hair and you'd be gorgeous.

LOGAN. Not gorgeous.

ALICIA. Sure. Change up the cut of your clothes, add a hair flip and Jaxton won't be able to keep his hands off you.

LOGAN. I've never understood the hair flip.

ALICIA. It's easy. You just flip.

(She does it. **LOGAN** tries to copy her.)

You've got it! It shows your neck. Makes guys want to kiss it.

(**LOGAN** recovers herself.)

LOGAN. OK. Enough hair flipping. What I want to tell you is that since LA, I quit acting because I realized that I could be so much more. I became a director so that I could show off the power of my mind. I'm a teacher so that I can change the future. I have plans, dreams. Jaxton has helped me stay focused on that path and I want to get you on it too.

ALICIA. My boyfriend helped me. But he dropped me from his agency so I dropped him from my life and moved out.

LOGAN. Good for you.

ALICIA. I mean if he's not getting me work then he's not getting sex. Right?

LOGAN. Um...there it is. You certainly should never feel pressured into sex or like it's a commodity.

ALICIA. Not unless I'm getting something good for it.

LOGAN. Well –

ALICIA. You've had sex, right?

LOGAN. Yes. But...you know what? As your employer we shouldn't even be talking about this. Now you're going to be a writer. You have so many more options for your future.

ALICIA. Look, I'm not that smart –

LOGAN. Don't say that.

ALICIA. No, really, I'm not. I've been tested. But I know how to make people stare at me and not look away. And when I say something on stage, people listen and they believe me. But this history stuff and writing, I don't know how to do that.

So if you want to make me feel empowered or whatever, let me do what I know how to do and don't force me to do something that makes me feel stupid.

LOGAN. But I am here to help you. Teach you.

ALICIA. I don't want to learn.

LOGAN. Seriously?

ALICIA. I'm happy doing my thing.

LOGAN. You have no ambition to be more than an actor?

ALICIA. What's wrong with being an actress?

LOGAN. Nothing. I just – I don't believe I've ever met a person without ambition. Not in any aspect of my life.

ALICIA. I'm ambitious. I want to do more acting.

LOGAN. Wow. You are certainly the most...simple person I've ever met.

ALICIA. I'm not smart but I'm definitely not simpleminded.

LOGAN. No. Simplicity is difficult. Multitasking, constantly trying to be something more, everyone does that. But to *be* simplicity, that's unbelievably difficult.

ALICIA. Not really. I just...don't do stuff I don't want to do and do the stuff I do.

LOGAN. You're talking directly to me and I can barely wrap my brain around it. I've never, for one moment in my life, been content.

ALICIA. I'm content all the time. Except when my agent dropped me but then I dumped him and felt fine.

LOGAN. Teach me how to be content.

ALICIA. Right now?

LOGAN. Please. You have no idea how stressed I am. But if I can get my reputation back with the parents and they withdraw that petition, next year I could – See, I'm doing it already. I'm already worried about next year's production and we just started this one. Help me be content with this moment I'm in. We're in, together.

ALICIA. Well, basically you don't do anything.

LOGAN. That's it?

ALICIA. Like normally in rehearsal if they are working on someone else's scene, I just sit here. Or play Angry Birds on my phone, but I forgot my charger so I don't want to wear down the battery.

LOGAN. So you meditate? Or think about...what?

ALICIA. Nothing. Sometimes I'll look out the window. Or I'll study the ceiling. People leave you alone when you study the ceiling.

LOGAN. OK.

ALICIA. So now we just do it.

LOGAN. Now?

ALICIA. Uh-huh.

> (**ALICIA** *sits back and stares at the ceiling.* **LOGAN** *studies her a bit then tries to do the same.*)

LOGAN. Do you count tiles or...

ALICIA. Nope, just stare at it.

LOGAN. Right.

> (**LOGAN** *struggles to keep staring.*)

I can't turn my brain off.

ALICIA. Maybe you're too smart to be content.

LOGAN. I am smart. I've been tested too.

ALICIA. I can tell.

LOGAN. So I can't be content?

ALICIA. I've never seen a smart person that is.

LOGAN. You're a lucky woman Alicia.

ALICIA. I think so.

LOGAN. You're also wise. You're sure you're not Native American?

ALICIA. Yep. Do you want me to work on my dream monologues?

LOGAN. No, you don't have to write anything.

ALICIA. Cool.

LOGAN. I need a break. Keep doing...nothing.

ALICIA. Got it.

> (**ALICIA** *resumes staring at the ceiling as* **LOGAN** *starts to go. The men return.*)

JAXTON. Logan, are there any swords in here?

LOGAN. No.

CADEN. Period rifles?

LOGAN. Nope.

CADEN. We'll have to make due.

> (**LOGAN** *goes as the men shuffle through papers.*)

Scene Five

*(Two actors sing as a period **WHITE PERSON** [pilgrim, western, etc.] and a **NATIVE**. Perhaps add additional songs in the style of "This Land is Your Land," etc.*)*

ACTOR 1. Youtube.com/eastsidemiddleschoolfortheperformingarts/thanksgivingassembly.

NATIVE. *(Tune: "Home on the Range.")*
OH GIVE ME A HOME WHERE THE BUFFALO ROAM,
WHERE THE DEER AND THE ANTELOPE PLAY,
WHERE SELDOM IS HEARD A DISCOURAGING WORD,
AND THE SKIES ARE NOT CLOUDY ALL DAY.

WHITE PERSON. *(Tune: "Home on the Range.")*
THE RED MAN WAS PRESSED
FROM THIS PART OF THE WEST,
HE'S LIKELY NO MORE TO RETURN,
TO THE BANKS OF THE RED RIVER
WHERE SELDOM IF EVER
THEIR FLICKERING CAMPFIRES BURN.

NATIVE. *(Tune: "My Country 'Tis of Thee.")*
MY COUNTRY 'TIS OF THEE,
SWEET LAND OF LIBERTY,
OF THEE I SING.
LAND WHERE MY FATHERS DIED!

WHITE PERSON. *(Tune: "My Country 'Tis of Thee.")*
LAND OF THE PILGRIMS' PRIDE!
FROM EVERY MOUNTAIN SIDE,

NATIVE & WHITE PERSON. Let freedom ring!

---

*A license to produce *The Thanksgiving Play* does not include a performance license for "This Land is Your Land." The publisher and author suggest that the licensee contact ASCAP or BMI to ascertain the music publisher and contact such music publisher to license or acquire permission for performance of the song. If a license or permission is unattainable for "This Land is Your Land," the licensee may not use the song in *The Thanksgiving Play* but should create an original composition in a similar style or use a similar song in the public domain. For further information, please see Music Use Note on page 3.

ACTOR 1. Public comment: Nine months ago. Are those really the lyrics? The "red man"? That's horrible.

ACTOR 2. Look it up, it's historical. Quit being so sensitive.

Scene Six

CADEN. But without the battle scene first –

JAXTON. Trust me, I think the real impact is in the scene after the battle. Back at the fort.

CADEN. Colony.

JAXTON. The Pilgrim Palace.

CADEN. Actually it was quite spartan.

JAXTON. Seriously man, you gotta loosen up on the facts.

CADEN. But facts are...facts. They don't loosen or tighten. They just are.

JAXTON. For now we gotta zero in on a compelling story, then we'll put all the facts in that you think we need, OK?

CADEN. Fine.

JAXTON. You've got a lot of scenes here.

CADEN. Thanks. Playwriting is a secret dream of mine.

JAXTON. You told us that in like the first two minutes.

CADEN. You're the only ones that know. And all of my students.

JAXTON. Gotta give voice to your dreams. Speak your truth and it will become truth.

CADEN. Well, I don't know that it actually works like –

JAXTON. Facts kill dreams.

CADEN. Well...

JAXTON. Do you know what I said I wanted to be when I grow up? An actor slash yoga dude.

CADEN. Like teach yoga?

JAXTON. Just be yoga. People told me that was crazy. It's not a "real" profession. But I said it anyway and here I am. I act and I do yoga. I spoke my truth. It became truth.

CADEN. That's seriously all you do?

JAXTON. Those are my passions.

CADEN. You get paid for your passions?

JAXTON. I have a day job, but that's not what's important in the story of me. Look, this homecoming scene of yours is the key.

CADEN. I don't think Logan will like it.

JAXTON. It's a devised piece. She doesn't have to like everything.

> (**LOGAN** *returns. Perhaps she has cleaned up a bit, added some lipstick. Something Alicia.*)

Lo, we've got a scene that has me so stoked.

LOGAN. Wow. That was fast. Great.

JAXTON. Cade's got like a whole play written. It just needs a little trimming and we could do it. Devising process done.

LOGAN. But what about our input?

CADEN. I can work in whatever Alicia's got.

ALICIA. Logan said I don't have to write anything. I'm being simplicity.

CADEN. Ummm...

LOGAN. I'm supporting Alicia in staying with her strengths. She knows what she does well and I want to honor that. It's so...brave and Zen really. Jaxton, she has absolutely no desire to be more. She's like you but way further down the path because she doesn't have intellect in her way.

JAXTON. Wait, like me?

LOGAN. Free. You yoga and sometimes act and just live. Alicia just acts. Nothing else.

ALICIA. I do do stuff. Sometimes.

LOGAN. But you don't *need* to do stuff. I'm telling you Jaxton. It's genius. Only she's not. That's not being offensive, she's been tested.

ALICIA. It's true.

LOGAN. I had it all wrong. She is here to mentor us.

JAXTON. Well, our scene is incredibly...simplicity. It strikes at the core of the Native American gestalt with one visual. It's quite brilliant.

CADEN. Thank you Jaxton.

JAXTON. There's lots of clunky educational dialogue but we'll fix that.

CADEN. Oh.

> (**JAXTON** *grabs his props: a bag with something large in it and various costume pieces. He nods to* **CADEN**.)

The year is 1631. Upon landing in Cape Cod the Separatists, now known as Pilgrims, immediately robbed the graves and nearly all of the food stores of the local Natives. However, with the help of Samoset, the English-speaking Native who had escaped slavery, a tenuous treaty was drawn. But, six years and many ships later, when the Separatists discovered a white man dead on a boat in Plymouth they assumed the Native people had killed him. Major John Mason –

> (**JAXTON** *steps forward.*)

gathered his men and surrounded an unsuspecting Pequot village. They killed four hundred Native men, women and children. Major Mason and his men came home to give thanks and celebrate their victory.

JAXTON. Do not fear good God-fearing folk. We have in short order laid waste to the savage villains. Prepare a feast most glorious and give thanks to God for he hath delivered our resounding victory. I bring forth the trophies of our labors.

> (*Out of his bag he pulls two crafted heads that have long, dark hair. They are oozing a red, blood-like liquid. He drops them on the ground. Blood sprays.*)

LOGAN. Wait. Are those heads?

CADEN. Native American heads.

JAXTON. We shall give sport with the heads of our enemies on this day of thanks.

CADEN. Yes we shall!

(JAXTON kicks a head to CADEN.)

LOGAN. Oh my God!

ALICIA. I wanna play!

(They ad-lib as they toss and kick the heads between them. Something is knocked over, LOGAN is horrified.)

LOGAN. Don't touch that Alicia!

ALICIA. Frozen Turkey Bowling!

(ALICIA jumps up and rolls a head into something. Heads fly around the stage, leaving blood everywhere.)

LOGAN. STOP!!

(They stop.)

Have you lost your minds? How is killing off hundreds of Indigenous people then kicking their heads a proper celebration of Native American Heritage Month?

CADEN. It's true, and gets a Native American presence into our play.

JAXTON. It's like those programs in high school where they make you visit a prison to stay out of prisons and see a crashed car to stay out of drunk driver cars and visit a morgue to…stay out of morgues.

LOGAN. This is appalling.

JAXTON. But it's real. That's what we need, not a cleansing of history but an in-your-face reminder that this is what we're capable of or we will keep doing it.

CADEN. Exactly.

LOGAN. If I do a gruesome play where you kick heads for sport, I will lose my job for sure.

JAXTON. But the genocide on Turtle Island is ongoing. If we white people don't admit the horrors of what we did and are still doing, it won't stop.

LOGAN. First off, this is public school, the growing majority of these kids aren't white anyway. Second, petition or

not, I will be fired. We aren't doing this. I'm the director.
I've decided.

JAXTON. Lo, it's devised theater.

LOGAN. Jaxton, I made it clear from the beginning that in
this format I will have final say.

JAXTON. Yeah but –

LOGAN. I said no!

JAXTON. You're being a bitch – bit dictatorial about it.

LOGAN. That is an incredibly offensive gender-biased
statement.

JAXTON. I went by the pronoun "they" for a full year. I'm
allowed one mistake.

LOGAN. That wasn't a mistake. You've always been jealous
of me because I'm a theater professional and you aren't.

JAXTON. You teach high school theater.

LOGAN. You are a street performer.

JAXTON. I'm a local celebrity.

ALICIA. Really?

LOGAN. Actually yes. But I believe that you, as a fellow
human, are having difficulty with the inequity of our
professional relationship and are lashing out.

> (**LOGAN** *executes a fantastic hair flip.* **ALICIA**
> *is proud.*)

ALICIA. Good girl.

> (**JAXTON** *has a realization.*)

JAXTON. Dude. I *am* feeling a tension in my positional
relationship to you.

LOGAN. I'm sorry I had to call it out like that.

JAXTON. Whoa. I think this is what "less than" feels like.

LOGAN. I don't think of you as less than me.

JAXTON. You called me a street performer.

LOGAN. Well, you are. But if saying it in that tone offended
you I am sorry for the results you felt even though that
wasn't my intention.

CADEN. I think it was.

JAXTON. It was. And that is a profound gift. Do you know how hard it is for a straight white male to feel "less than" in this world? I don't know that I've ever truly felt it in my life.

CADEN. I have.

JAXTON. I don't want to lose this feeling. Say it again.

LOGAN. Seriously?

JAXTON. Please, help me Lo.

LOGAN. Um...you're a street performer?

JAXTON. Come on, give it to me.

LOGAN. You're a street performer.

JAXTON. If you care about me, hit me with it.

LOGAN. You're a bad street performer!

JAXTON. Yes!

LOGAN. The school board said I didn't have to hire you but you work for free!

JAXTON. More!

LOGAN. You're a terrible actor.

JAXTON. Hurt me!

LOGAN. And the sex is so –

JAXTON. Back off!

LOGAN. Bizarre! Why do you do –

JAXTON. Too far!

LOGAN. Sorry!

JAXTON. I should go meditate on this feeling right now.

LOGAN. Should we talk about...

> (**JAXTON** *sits to meditate.*)

JAXTON. OMMMMMM.

LOGAN. Maybe we should all meditate for a moment.

ALICIA. Umm...

LOGAN. Just keep doing nothing.

ALICIA. Got it.

(**LOGAN** *and* **JAXTON** *take meditation positions.* **ALICIA** *sits back and stares at the ceiling.*)

(**CADEN** *isn't sure what to do. He tries an asana, not great. Finally, he sits in a chair and puts his head down on a desk.*)

Scene Seven

*(The agitprop version. Don't get too earnest,
let the appropriation fly.)*

ACTOR. Applying social responsibility and ethics to a classroom Thanksgiving. Lesson plan for grades nine through twelve.

ALL. Where?

Plymouth Massachusetts.

When?

Thanksgiving 1997.

Who?

The United American Indians of New England.
And the local police.

What?

Since 1970 a National Day of Mourning has been observed with a march at noon.

In 1997 police attempted to disband the march with tear gas and violent arrests.

Twenty-five people were arrested, many injured.

Medical attention was not immediately provided to those under arrest.

The police characterized the protesters as "terrorists" who should be treated accordingly.

Why?

(Silence.)

ACTOR. Final assignment: Have students write letters of apology to the Indians. Then, read them to each other.

Scene Eight

LOGAN. I've got it! Sorry. When you folx are done.

CADEN. I'm good.

ALICIA. Whatever.

JAXTON. Om.

LOGAN. We'll start and Jaxton can join us. I want to try a Pilgrim-style Thanksgiving scene but we show the actual erasure of Native people. Graphically.

CADEN. I thought the scene with the heads was pretty graphic.

LOGAN. Graphic in a visceral way, not a visual one. We do a First Thanksgiving scene, like normal with Native people, but we don't play Native people. We allow their absence to speak for them. Where is the missing Indigenous perspective? It's certainly missing from this room. We hold space for them by literally holding space for them. Give me a few minutes to work out some dialogue.

CADEN. I have a dinner scene I was holding onto. No death or Spaniards. Just the "normal" story we all know.

LOGAN. Let me see it.

(**CADEN** *looks through a large stack.*)

You actually wrote the whole play didn't you?

CADEN. There's nothing that means more to me in my life than this opportunity.

LOGAN. Thanks for this work. All of it Caden.

CADEN. Here it is!

(*He hands* **LOGAN** *a scene.*)

LOGAN. Everyone take a break while I figure this out.

(**LOGAN** *goes somewhere to work on it.*)

(**JAXTON** *joins* **CADEN** *and* **ALICIA** *at the snacks.*)

JAXTON. That meditation was deep. I faced a lot about myself and my privilege.

CADEN. I don't know if I could hear my girlfriend say that kind of stuff about me and be OK with it.

JAXTON. I know that her lashing out is not about her and me but actually her double Xs fighting back against centuries of patriarchal oppression. It's not personal. It felt personal for a second, which I totally needed, but intellectually I know to filter anything she says to me through layers of justified feminine rage.

CADEN. So no matter what she says, you don't believe it?

JAXTON. I believe she believes it, but I know to trust myself first. And not everyone is ready for Tantric, right?
(*To* **ALICIA.**) You play oppressed characters a lot, how do you get in touch with that as a person of privilege?

ALICIA. I imagine I'm that character so I feel what they feel.

JAXTON. But do you use substitution technique from your own life or method or what?

ALICIA. I pretend to be them.

JAXTON. That's it?

ALICIA. Yeah. And I can make myself cry on command.

JAXTON. Like in a scene?

ALICIA. No. Right now.

(**ALICIA** *literally cries tears.*)

JAXTON. Whoa.

CADEN. That is impressive.

(*She stops.*)

ALICIA. I list it on my special skills. People ask me to do it in auditions all the time.

JAXTON. I'm getting what Logan was saying about you. You're so...simple.

ALICIA. She called me simplicity.

JAXTON. That's it. You should teach workshops. People would dig that.

ALICIA. It seems like either you have simplicity or you don't. Smart people don't get it. I just tried with Logan and she couldn't do it.

JAXTON. So I'm probably too smart?

ALICIA. Maybe. He is for sure.

CADEN. I'm OK with that.

JAXTON. But still, you could charge people money to come listen to you.

ALICIA. That's what I do now. I'm an actress.

JAXTON. You are blowing my mind. Seriously. Mind blown.

ALICIA. No one's ever said that to me before when I had my clothes on.

> *(JAXTON and CADEN register this.)*

JAXTON. I can't formulate a response that isn't not misogynistic.

ALICIA. Simplicity.

> *(LOGAN rejoins them.)*

LOGAN. OK, this is experimental but that's what I love about theater for kids. You can really do anything and they will follow you. We'll sit around the table of the first Thanksgiving. Our Native friends are at the end.

> *(They arrange chairs and sit with two empty chairs.)*

First time through let's read all the lines. I'll read both Samoset and Massasoit.

> *(She moves back and forth between the chairs as she does Samoset's or Massasoit's lines. CADEN tends to mouth the words along with them.)*

ALICIA. Good Native king and good interpreter, welcome on this day of the good Lord's Feast of Thanksgiving. What may I offer to make your visit pleasing?

LOGAN. I Samoset whilst request more of the fowl your men gathered with their exploding sticks.

ALICIA. Wouldest thou prefer the breast or the leg?

LOGAN. Massasoit, which part of the bird is most pleasing to your countenance?

(Switching chairs as Massasoit.) That which is most succulent pleaseth me.

ALICIA. The breast is ample whilst the leg is moist.

JAXTON. Dear wife, our gratitude is owed these men a thousand times. Please, take the whole between you.

CADEN. Yes, we wouldest have died as did so many of our number.

LOGAN. Scene. Great work everyone.

> **(CADEN** *is overcome with emotion or heartburn.)*

JAXTON. Dude, are you OK?

CADEN. It just hit me. I read my words with real actors. This is the best day of my life!

JAXTON. Most people go their whole lives without living their dreams, but you put yourself out there.

LOGAN. I'm thrilled to facilitate this moment for you Caden. I'd like to take a second to honor your emotional space.

> *(They all do.)*

And do it again.

CADEN. It would help to hear it with better acting this time. *(To* **JAXTON** *and* **ALICIA.***)* I think some context of why you two are so grateful might help you get the emotional arc –

JAXTON. Not cool.

LOGAN. Caden, it's customary that actors do not give each other notes. Any notes come through the director.

CADEN. Just trying to be helpful. There was something missing last time.

ALICIA. Want me to cry at the end?

CADEN. That would be great.

LOGAN. OK. Let's read it again and see what happens. This time when we get to the Native lines, I won't read them but we look at the space and listen as if the Native characters are there.

ALICIA. But they aren't.

LOGAN. We're pretending.

ALICIA. Oh. I can do that.

Good Native king and good interpreter, welcome on this day of the good Lord's Feast of Thanksgiving. What may I offer to make your visit pleasing?

> *(They look to a chair in silence. **ALICIA** can't help but go sex-kittenish. It's a reflex. The group's attention is drawn to her like moths to a flame.)*

Wouldest thou prefer the breast or the leg?

> *(Silence again.)*

The breast is ample whilst the leg is moist.

> *(**JAXTON** bursts into giggles.)*

What?

JAXTON. Ample breast, moist legs?

> *(**ALICIA** laughs.)*

CADEN. Only those with juvenile humor would find this pleasant exchange about food humorous.

JAXTON. Our audience is all juveniles.

LOGAN. *Juvenile* humor aside, I think it really worked. Notice how in the moments of silence, we were all totally focused. It was so impactful.

ALICIA. I felt that.

JAXTON. But can we do a whole play like that?

LOGAN. It's applicable to our contemporary situation. Erased presence.

CADEN. Although the acting was great. It wasn't as strong for me as the first time with all of the lines.

LOGAN. This is very early discovery, we're playing.

CADEN. Perhaps we could do it like a ventriloquist. Still keep the visual nothingness but say their lines. Like this. *(Poorly done ventriloquist voice.)* I Samoset whilst request more of the fowl your men gathered with their exploding sticks.

JAXTON. *(Giggling.)* Exploding sticks. Caden, you horny man. You wrote a sex comedy.

CADEN. I did not!

LOGAN. Please stop talking about sex.

JAXTON. I'm simply naming what's in the room.

LOGAN. It's a children's show.

JAXTON. Caden wrote a sex comedy. And I, as a heteronormative male, recognize and honor the power of Alicia's sacral chakra.

(*To* **ALICIA.**) Oh yeah, I'll give you something to feast on.

(**ALICIA** *catches on and plays the part.*)

ALICIA. Partake of my generous bounty good sir.

JAXTON. Let your rich sauces run down my chin.

ALICIA. Whilst thou have me carve the breast?

JAXTON. Wait, what?

LOGAN. That's enough. Caden, the voice takes away from the idea of erased presence. Know what I mean?

CADEN. I don't think the erased presence works as well as the lines I wrote.

JAXTON. He's right Lo, the silence is wrong.

LOGAN. Why are you fighting me?

JAXTON. By silencing the Native voices we've made them too strong. Silence is so powerful onstage. Our characters can't compete with that.

LOGAN. But we want the silence to be strong. The nothingness of the Natives is the whole point.

JAXTON. So it's an inequality.

LOGAN. Yes.

JAXTON. Then are we being fair to the Pilgrims?

CADEN. Separatists.

JAXTON. White people.

LOGAN. Aren't we aiming for an equitable world, not a fair world?

JAXTON. You've hit it right in the chakras. By doing this with the silenced voices, we are reinforcing the inequality of humans. Calling out one human as more worthy of attention and power.

LOGAN. But it is Native American Heritage Month. A particular time specified to lift up one people's voice over others.

JAXTON. But do we believe in that or have we played right into a massive blind spot? If you make a month for everyone, will it ever be fair? No. Someone will always be left out. Or get a weird month like Hispanic Heritage Month.

ALICIA. When's Hispanic Heritage Month?

JAXTON. September 15 to October 15.

ALICIA. How is that even a month?

JAXTON. Exactly.

LOGAN. Well it is thirty days.

CADEN. And it coincides with the Independence days of several Latin American countries.

JAXTON. Come on, how is it equal to give one group a mid-month as their month?

ALICIA. There isn't a white person month. I checked.

JAXTON. That's what I'm saying. Thank you Alicia.

LOGAN. Basically every month is white person month.

JAXTON. But once we are the minority again, will we get an official month? And will that make things right? No. The point is, this whole project is inherently inequitable. By raising up one voice through a month or silence, we are lowering another. That's not what we should be teaching children.

LOGAN. I think we're getting off track. My idea –

JAXTON. We have a worksheet for this. To add up privilege so that we can then equalize it.

ALICIA. What is privilege?

LOGAN. The things about you that give you power.

ALICIA. I'm hot. That's power so that's privilege.

LOGAN. Believing your power is only because of your looks is buying into a subjective social construct.

ALICIA. I haven't opened a door or paid for a drink since I was sixteen. Hotness is privilege.

CADEN. I think she's right.

LOGAN. Although I respect your hotness, this talk will get my Go! Girls! Scholastic Leadership funding pulled.

JAXTON. We can talk about your hotness at break Alicia. Now if we apply the worksheet to Logan's idea...

(He works it out on a chalk or whiteboard.)

The white people are visible so that's one point. The Native people have a month and silence so that's two points. The story is written pretty evenly so that's a point to both. See, the silence makes it unequal.

(ALICIA studies the math.)

ALICIA. So if one side is silent, to make it equal don't both sides have to be silent?

JAXTON. She might be right. It is the definition of simplicity.

CADEN. No it's not. It's the definition of madness. You can't have a silent play.

JAXTON. Actually, it's been done.

CADEN. How will they hear my script?

JAXTON. They were only going to hear the white half anyway. This would be closer to equal.

CADEN. What do we do, mime the story of the first Thanksgiving?

ALICIA. Mimes are so rude.

JAXTON. I think we just...feel the words.

ALICIA. I can do that.

LOGAN. Fine, let's give it a try.

CADEN. No.

LOGAN. Caden, it's a fluid process. It doesn't mean we are abandoning script completely.

CADEN. Yes it does. You've talked yourselves into this equality thing. I have written sixty-two plays for grown-ups and this is the first one that has been read by actors over the age of nine. Do you have any idea how hard it is to labor over every line of historically correct language then only hear them read by people who can't read three-syllable words? It's excruciating. This is finally my chance to have my words read by people who can spell "theater."

ALICIA. It's "R-E" right?

CADEN. That's a very interesting debate that I'll tell you about later. But right now I'm not letting you take away my chance to have my words read by grown-ups.

JAXTON. It's the right thing to do. Go Alicia.

> (**ALICIA** *jumps right into sexy Pilgrim poses.*)

CADEN. I can't go back to third grade! I won't!

> (**JAXTON** *joins* **ALICIA** *in the silent scene.*)

Good Native king and good interpreter!

JAXTON. Respect the math Caden.

> (*The following action moves quickly, overlapping lines.*)

CADEN. Welcome on this day of –

JAXTON. Shhh.

CADEN. The good Lord's Feast of –

JAXTON. Shut it.

CADEN. Thanksgiving.

> (**JAXTON** *puts his hand over* **CADEN**'s *mouth.*)

LOGAN. Respectful touch. Respectful touch.

CADEN. *(Muffled.)* What may I offer…

> (**CADEN** *escapes* **JAXTON**.)

To make your visit pleasing?

> (*It becomes a comedic scuffle, two non-fighters.* **ALICIA** *joins their scuffle while being sexy and silent except to interject squeals or concern.*)

LOGAN. Alicia, please stop that.

JAXTON. Don't push me Caden.

CADEN. I Samoset request the fowl your men gathered –

LOGAN. Think about the kids!

CADEN. With their exploding sticks! Massasoit, which part of the bird is most pleasing to your countenance? That which is most succulent pleaseth me.

JAXTON. You're ruining the simplicity!

LOGAN. We are the future!

CADEN. The breast is ample –

JAXTON. That's it.

(*JAXTON tries to stop* **CADEN** *one final time.*)

CADEN. Whilst the leg is moist!

LOGAN. Everyone just stop doing anything!!

(*Everyone freezes in a weird physical moment.*)

(*Once they have settled,* **LOGAN** *notices the empty center of the room.*)

We've done it.

JAXTON. This?

LOGAN. In the middle of the room. Look at it.

(*Everyone looks.*)

CADEN. What?

ALICIA. I don't see it.

LOGAN. That is our play.

CADEN. I'm not following.

LOGAN. That space in the middle. That perfectly equitable emptiness.

ALICIA. I wanna see.

CADEN. The room is the play?

LOGAN. We've been trying too hard. The *empty space* is completely, finally equal. That is our Thanksgiving play.

CADEN. So the entire play is "nothingness"?

ALICIA. Oh, I see *that.*

LOGAN. Four white people can't do a play about Thanksgiving that doesn't piss off the funders or the parents or the universe. So we don't. Feel it for a moment.

(They do.)

ALICIA. I feel it!

CADEN. It is...something.

JAXTON. This nothing breaks the cycle of lies, stereotypes and inequality.

CADEN. The parents can't object to that.

JAXTON. It's brilliant Lo. You did it.

LOGAN. No, we did it. We all created this nothing together.

(They appreciate their accomplishment.)

JAXTON. So we're done!

CADEN. That's it?

LOGAN. One rehearsal. That's got to be a record.

JAXTON. That's how us professionals roll.

ALICIA. But I think I have a contract to act in a play.

LOGAN. You and Jaxton will still be credited as actors and collaborators. Caden will have an added credit of dramaturg.

*(**CADEN** inhales sharply, instantly emotional.)*

CADEN. Dramaturg? The holy grail of American theater titles.

ALICIA. What is that?

CADEN. No one knows.

ALICIA. I still get paid for the rest of the rehearsals, right?

LOGAN. Of course.

CADEN. Can we come back tomorrow?

LOGAN. We don't have to. But the space is here for us if we want it.

CADEN. We could work on the sex comedy.

ALICIA. I'd like that.

(She throws her version of a sex comedy into the room.)

LOGAN. As the director I should technically be in the room.

CADEN. So, same time tomorrow? I'll bring pages.

ALICIA. I'll be late. Just…because.

CADEN. Because of the bus?

ALICIA. Oh right. That's why.

CADEN. I could give you a ride home. And pick you up. And give you a ride home again.

(ALICIA considers him.)

ALICIA. OK. Can you also write a play for me? I want to portray a better-known historical feminist woman like Carrie Bradshaw. Or Lara Croft. Or Shakira.

CADEN. Sure.

(ALICIA and CADEN go. Quick goodbyes all around.)

(LOGAN offers the recoupling gesture. JAXTON joins her.)

LOGAN. Are we OK?

JAXTON. Yeah. You've inspired me Lo, really.

LOGAN. Thank you. That means a lot.

JAXTON. This piece, the nothing. It's taught me that we need to do more of that.

LOGAN. How can the play be more than nothing?

JAXTON. Not the play. We need to be less. Do less. That's the lesson. By doing nothing, we become part of the solution. But it has to start here, with us.

LOGAN. Yes.

(They appreciate the nothing a moment more.)

(Lights out. The center of the room remains lit but empty.)

End of Play